CW01512500

Original title:

Netted Tones Beyond the Elf Bower

Copyright © 2025 Swan Charm

Author: Sebastian Sarapuu

ISBN HARDBACK: 978-1-80559-321-8

ISBN PAPERBACK: 978-1-80559-820-6

The Songbirds' Secret

In the dawn, they softly sing,
Whispers of a joyful spring.
Feathers bright, hearts so free,
Secrets shared among the trees.

Melodies that dance in the air,
Echoing love, beyond compare.
Each note a kiss, a tender plea,
Binding souls in harmony.

Tones from the Enchanted Brook

Rippling waters, crystal clear,
Calling forth the heart to hear.
Nature's voice, gentle and light,
Guiding wanderers through the night.

Beneath the stars, the brook does sing,
A lullaby from Earth's own spring.
Tales of old in every flow,
Whispers of the world below.

Echoes of the Dreaming Thicket

In the thicket, shadows play,
Dreams of night fade with the day.
Mystic visions cast their spell,
Every echo, a story to tell.

Softly rustling, leaves entwine,
Cradling secrets, lush and fine.
An invitation, lost in time,
To wander where the spirits climb.

Tidal Vows of the Mystic Glade

Waves that break upon the shore,
Whisper vows forevermore.
In moonlit glow, the tides embrace,
Every ripple, a soft trace.

In the glade where flowers bloom,
Love's sweet scent dispels all gloom.
Nature's heart beats wild and strong,
In the tide, we all belong.

Celestial Whispers Through Verdant Veils

In the glade where shadows twine,
Stars spill light, their soft design.
Leaves dance gently, secrets sway,
Nature's breath in quiet play.

Moonlight tinged with silver grace,
Kisses each and every place.
Whispers weave through branches high,
Soft as echoes, drifting by.

Breezes carry tales of old,
In the night, their warmth unfolds.
Celestial songs, a timeless call,
Calling forth the night to fall.

With each rustle, spirits near,
Breath of starlight, crisp and clear.
Veils of green embrace the dark,
Crickets sing their evening lark.

In this realm where shadows blend,
Whispers linger, never end.
Hearts attune to nature's sigh,
Celestial realms draw nigh.

Songs of the Ancient Ones in the Gloom

In the depths where silence cleaves,
Echoes from the ancient leaves.
Chanting low, their voices soar,
Wisdom shared from yesteryore.

With the dusk, their tales arise,
Underneath the shrouded skies.
Rustling softly, whispers weave,
Songs of elders, dusk believe.

In the shadows, roots entwine,
Binding stories, yours and mine.
Breath of earth and sky collide,
In the gloom, where dreams abide.

Murmurs painting twilight's grace,
Soft reminders in this place.
Binding time with tendrils strong,
Ancient rhythms, time's own song.

As the stars begin to weep,
Secrets in the silence seep.
Gloom may hold what we forget,
Songs of old, we won't regret.

Melodic Footsteps Through the Fairy Domain

In the glen where fairies tread,
Silken paths of light are spread.
Joyful notes on breezes flow,
Melodies of tales we know.

Dancing through the petals bright,
Glimmers twirl in pure delight.
Whispers twine with every flight,
Footsteps echo through the night.

Underneath the moon's soft gaze,
Secrets wrapped in silver haze.
Every laugh a tuneful spell,
Melodies that weave and swell.

Through the ferns and mossy glades,
Harmony that never fades.
Bubbles burst in laughter's game,
In this world, we know their names.

With each step, enchantments rise,
Charming hearts beneath the skies.
Fairy songs, both sweet and bold,
In the twilight, tales retold.

The Spirit of Melody Among the Ferns

In the forest where ferns grow,
Softest notes begin to flow.
Nature hums in gentle tones,
Melodies made of earth and stones.

Each frond sways with painted grace,
Whispering through this vibrant space.
Rustling softly, spirits play,
Calling forth the close of day.

With every breeze, a song reborn,
Echoes dance, no heart forlorn.
Laughter mingles with the sighs,
In this realm, pure magic lies.

Among the roots and ancient trees,
Rhythms ride upon the breeze.
Notes entwined with every shade,
Harmony in twilight laid.

Here the spirit melds with light,
In the ferns, our hearts take flight.
Melody where silence dwells,
In this realm, the music swells.

Celestial Notes in the Sylvan Air

In the quiet woods, whispers rise,
Melodies dance under vast skies.
Golden rays play on forest floors,
Nature's song through open doors.

Gentle winds carry sweet refrains,
Echoes of life in sunlit lanes.
Birds weave tunes in leafy heights,
Their voices soar, a pure delight.

Rustling leaves join in the score,
Every branch sings, a tale of yore.
Dreams linger where shadows blend,
In twilight hours, songs ascend.

Moonlight glimmers on silver streams,
Softly weaving through our dreams.
The nightingale's lullabies flow,
A celestial bath in soft glow.

Harmony bathes the sylvan scene,
Nature's heart beats, calm and serene.
With each note, the spirit takes flight,
In the woods, all feels just right.

Spirits' Aria Beneath the Starry Veil

Under the stars, whispers awake,
With the night, a sacred pact we make.
Luminous skies, a celestial dance,
Draw us closer in a mystic trance.

Ghostly figures in twilight roam,
Their spectral songs beckon us home.
With every note, the ancients call,
Their stories echo, a shroud of thrall.

In the hush of night, spirits conspire,
Painting darkness with whispered fire.
Beneath the moon, shadows entwine,
Their harmonies echo, so divine.

Crescent dreams play in the night air,
Each note a wish, a whispered prayer.
Stars align, their secrets to hear,
In their glow, we shed our fear.

The aria swells, a ghostly choir,
Entwines our hearts in love's desire.
Beneath the veil, we are set free,
Among the stars, we find the key.

Rhythms of the Enchanted Hidden Path

Amidst the woods, secrets unfold,
Every step whispers tales untold.
Winding trails in emerald shades,
Lead us where enchantment pervades.

Mossy carpets underfoot lay,
Guiding dreams on their gentle sway.
The echoes of nature drum the tune,
Calling forth the silver moon.

In twilight's embrace, shadows prance,
Curtains of leaves weave the dance.
Each rustle, a pulse in this place,
Rhythms quicken, our hearts race.

The fragrance of earth, rich and deep,
Awakens the magic, makes us leap.
In the air, a melody sings,
Of whispers shared from ancient kings.

Paths entwined in the forest's embrace,
Lead to wonders time can't erase.
With every beat, we find our way,
Through enchanted realms where fairies play.

Nature's Symphony Beneath the Tree Canopy

Beneath the trees, a symphony grows,
Each leaf a note, as the soft wind blows.
Branches sway to the rhythm of life,
A harmony born of joy and strife.

Squirrels scurry, their chatter cascades,
In this orchestra where peace pervades.
Crickets chirp under twilight's dome,
Their music invites the weary home.

Streams gurgle with laughter and cheer,
A gentle lullaby for all to hear.
In this haven, the heart finds rest,
Nature's embrace is truly the best.

The sun dips low, casting gold rays,
Lighting up the symphony's plays.
In every rustle, in every sound,
The pulse of life waits to be found.

From dawn's first light to dusk's soft sigh,
Nature's symphony weaves through the sky.
In her solace, we're never alone,
For beneath the trees, we've found our home.

Sibilant Secrets of the Eldritch Woods

Whispers dance among the trees,
Breath of shadows in the breeze.
Glimmers hide where minds can't peek,
Mystic echoes softly speak.

Ancient roots and twisting lore,
Guard the tales of ages worn.
Footfalls lost in twilight's hush,
Silent secrets, wild and lush.

In the thicket, sighs entwine,
Nature's song, a thread divine.
Moonlit paths of silken fears,
Where the past in silence nears.

Creatures lurking, eyes aglow,
In the deep where few dare go.
Sibilant whispers weave their sound,
Life's enigmas all around.

And though the night may cast its veil,
In the woods, the spirits sail.
To hear their secrets, one must seek,
In the silence, truth can speak.

Luminescent Pathways of Sound

Echoes shimmer in the night,
Softly glowing with delight.
Each step whispers tales untold,
In the dark, the dreams unfold.

Crystal notes from hidden streams,
Chasing softly, fragile dreams.
Breezes hum their timeless tune,
Guiding hearts beneath the moon.

Footfalls glow on winding trails,
Carried forth by gentle gales.
Every sound, a soul's embrace,
Lighting up the world's vast space.

Stars above in harmony,
Resonate with destiny.
Silent wishes float like sighs,
On this path where music lies.

In the echoes, life is spun,
Underneath the night's great sun.
Luminescent pathways found,
In the silence, all is sound.

Reverberations of a Hidden Sanctuary

In the glen where shadows play,
Echoes drift and softly sway.
Whispers weave through trees so tall,
Nature's voice, a sacred call.

Hushed tones linger in the air,
Filling hearts with ancient care.
In this peace, the world stands still,
Time suspends, a tranquil thrill.

Pulsing rhythms mark the ground,
In the stillness, peace is found.
Voices blend with rustling leaves,
In this space, the spirit breathes.

Ethereal sights where patterns flow,
Guiding seekers, hearts aglow.
Every sigh, a gentle guide,
In this calm, the soul confides.

Reverberate through wood and stone,
Nature's heart, forever known.
In the sanctuary's warm light,
Lost in echoes, pure delight.

Serenade of the Fairy Hearth

Beneath the stars, the fairies play,
Dancing through the night, they sway.
With a song of dreams so sweet,
Whirls of magic, hearts will meet.

Crickets chirp in harmony,
Joining in the revelry.
Glittering wings as soft as air,
Fill the night with twinkling flair.

By the hearth, the warmth ablaze,
Holding spells of ancient days.
Stories weave through laughter light,
In this cozy, endless night.

Flickers shine like fireflies bright,
Illuminating pure delight.
Every giggle, every cheer,
Echoes of joy, crystal clear.

In this realm where wishes grow,
Life's enchantments all will flow.
Serenade of hearts that yearn,
In the hearth, we brightly burn.

Whispers of the Enchanted Grove

In shadows deep, the ancients sigh,
Where secrets dwell, beneath the sky.
The leaves will dance, the breezes hum,
In whispered tones, the night will come.

With every step, the magic stirs,
A symphony in nature's purrs.
The owls awake, the nightingale,
Their melodies weave a haunting tale.

Beneath the boughs, the fairies play,
In twinkling lights, they dart away.
The moon looks down, with silver beams,
Illuminating our wildest dreams.

The brook does babble, a soothing song,
Where creatures roam and night feels long.
Each rustling leaf, a call to hear,
In this enchanted grove, so dear.

So linger here, let worries fade,
Among the magic that nature made.
For in this space, time stands still,
In whispers soft, our souls it fills.

Secret Lullabies in the Faerie Glade

In twilight's hush, the glade awakes,
As moonlight weaves through ancient oaks.
With petals soft, the faeries sing,
A lullaby that sweetly clings.

The stars emerge, like diamonds bright,
As echoes twirl in the soft night.
With whispered dreams, they float on air,
In gentle tones, beyond compare.

The flowers sway, with secrets shared,
A world of wonder, softly bared.
Through silver streams, their laughter flows,
In quiet corners, love still glows.

Each note a balm, for restless souls,
The faerie glade, a place that consoles.
With every breeze, a story spun,
In secret tunes of moon and sun.

So close your eyes, let sleep embrace,
The lullabies of this sacred space.
Let dreams take flight, unfurl your heart,
In faerie glades, where magic starts.

Twilight Serenades of the Sylvan Realm

Beneath the arch of twilight's veil,
The sylvan realm begins to sail.
With secret chords, the nightbirds cheer,
A serenade for all to hear.

The trees in concert, bending low,
As starlit whispers begin to flow.
In golden hues, the shadows play,
While gentle breezes find their way.

Through tangled roots, the echoes rise,
Unveiling tales beneath the skies.
A harmony of night and day,
In twilight's glow, they softly sway.

The softest sigh of passing leaves,
A call to dream, as the heart believes.
With every pulse, the forest beats,
In serenades, where magic meets.

So linger long in this embrace,
The twilight calls with tender grace.
Let nature's voice uplift your soul,
In sylvan realms, you will be whole.

Echoes of the Moonlit Canopy

Beneath the moon, a silver screen,
The canopy of dreams is seen.
With shadows dancing, life unfolds,
In whispers soft, the night beholds.

The owls will hoot, the crickets chime,
As nature's pulse beats in its prime.
In every rustle, a story dwells,
Of ancient magic, woven spells.

The branches sway, like lullabies,
As starlit wonders fill the skies.
With every rustle, secrets bloom,
In echoes sweet, dispelling gloom.

The breeze carries a gentle sigh,
Reminding us that dreams can fly.
In moonlit balm, we find our peace,
Where echoes linger, sorrows cease.

So look above, and hear the call,
In moonlit canopies, we fall.
For in this night, all hearts unite,
In echoes soft, pure and bright.

Aria of the Glade's Infinite Secrets

In the heart of quiet woods,
Secrets hum with every breeze.
Leaves whisper tales of ages past,
Beneath the ancient, towering trees.

Moonlight dances on the stream,
Illuminating paths of gold.
Nature keeps her mysteries,
In stories softly told.

Flowers bloom in vibrant hues,
They beckon all who wander near.
With petals kissed by morning dew,
They sing, revealing what we fear.

Shadows stretch as daylight fades,
While crickets start their song anew.
In the glade, where magic sways,
The night unveils a wondrous view.

Every rustle holds a truth,
Every chime of bellflower bright.
In the glade's eternal dance,
Secrets dwell beneath the light.

Fables sung by the Whispering Winds

Winds carry tales from distant lands,
Through valleys deep and mountains high.
They weave their lore with gentle hands,
In softest breezes passing by.

Leaves flutter softly, secrets shared,
With each caress, a story spun.
Nature's breath, forever aired,
In timeless fables, never done.

From pine and oak, the wisdom flows,
Of trials faced and battles fought.
In echoes of the past, it grows,
A tapestry of lessons taught.

With every gust, a truth revealed,
As nature sings her soothing tune.
In the heart, the pain is healed,
By whispers soft beneath the moon.

So heed the winds that swirl around,
Their gentle notes invite you near.
For in their song, the world is found,
In woven tales, both brave and clear.

Echoing Footsteps in the Glistening Moss

Through emerald paths, the silence hums,
With every step, the glistening calls.
Footprints whispered on soft moss drums,
In nature's hall, where beauty sprawls.

Each stride a promise of what is near,
In iridescent drops, hope glows.
Mossy carpets cradle fear,
While sunlight weaves through bending bows.

Echoing footsteps of those before,
In harmony with nature's beat.
Their stories linger evermore,
In every rise and rhythmic feet.

The forest holds its breath in awe,
As shadows stretch and twilight sighs.
Reflective ponds, nature's mirror draw,
Revealing the balance of lows and highs.

In each soft thud, the forest breathes,
Embracing all who dare to roam.
With grateful hearts, the spirit weaves,
A welcoming path that feels like home.

Harmonic Dances of the Nature Spirits

In twilight's glow, the spirits sway,
To melodies of leaf and breeze.
Nature's ballet, vibrant display,
As starlight sparkles through the trees.

With every twirl, the glades come alive,
In symphonies of rustling leaves.
Harmony beckons all to thrive,
Where magic lingers and belief weaves.

Fireflies twinkle in the night,
Guiding the dance with flickering light.
Each spirit twirls, embracing the glow,
In a world where wonders overflow.

As the moon casts shadows wide and deep,
The rhythm of nature takes its flight.
A sacred space for souls to leap,
In joyous laughter, pure delight.

So come and join the endless prance,
With nature spirits in gentle flight.
In every heartbeat, take a chance,
To dance with dreams beneath the night.

Fanciful Echoes of Wonderland

In a realm where shadows play,
Colors swirl and dance all day.
Whispers echo, secrets found,
Magic lingers all around.

Wonders bloom in every glance,
Forest creatures twirl and prance.
Curious paths lead us to
Dreams that cast a world anew.

Laughter weaves through leaves and air,
Songs of joy, beyond compare.
Here in wonder, hearts ignite,
In the glow of pure delight.

Moonlit glades where wishes soar,
Glimmers bright on every shore.
Echoes of a timeless lore,
Fanciful, forevermore.

Twilight's Touch on the Harmony of Trees

As day fades into shadows deep,
Whispers of the night begin to creep.
Each leaf sighs in gentle tone,
Nature's symphony, widely known.

Twilight's brush paints skies in hues,
Softly blending dark with blues.
Branches sway, a lullaby,
Underneath the starry sky.

In this moment, time stands still,
Hearts attune to nature's will.
A dance of dusk, a sweet embrace,
Harmony found in every space.

Echoing life, serene and wise,
Voices mingle with the sighs.
Where the forest holds its breath,
At twilight's grace, defying death.

Dreamlike Reverie Among the Blossoms

In fields of hue, where dreams are sown,
Petals float, as hope has grown.
Sweet fragrance swirls, a gentle tease,
Nature's gift, a heart's reprise.

Minds take flight on blossoms' dance,
Each bud holding a fleeting chance.
In the hush, a secret blooms,
Within the heart, a feeling looms.

Laughter echoes, soft and bright,
Sunshine weaves its golden light.
Whispers in the breeze do sing,
Joyful notes that spring can bring.

Amidst the blooms, lost in sight,
Dreamlike visions take their flight.
In this reverie, we find peace,
Among the blossoms, worries cease.

Enchanted Harmonies in the Dappled Light

Through the trees, the sunlight weaves,
Whispers twine like gentle leaves.
Dappled light on forest floor,
Enchanting hearts forevermore.

Notes of birds in joyful tune,
Echo softly, 'neath the moon.
Nature's choir fills the air,
Every note, a breath laid bare.

In the glade, where shadows play,
Harmony guides the night to stay.
Each heartbeat aligns with the sound,
In this magic, peace is found.

Winds caress and softly sway,
Telling tales through night and day.
With every rustle, every sigh,
Enchanted dreams begin to fly.

Songs Carried by the Evening Breeze

Whispers soft through leaves aglow,
A melody that starts to flow.
The nightingale begins to sing,
In harmony with twilight's wing.

Stars emerge in velvet skies,
While distant echoes gently rise.
The breeze picks up the fading light,
Cocooning all within the night.

Luna dances on a beam,
Silvery notes in moonlit dream.
Each sigh of wind, a tender plea,
Carried forth, a symphony.

In shadows deep, lost tales reside,
Of laughter shared, by flameside.
With every note, a story spun,
A gentle kiss from day to done.

So listen close and let it be,
The songs that float on twilight's sea.
In fleeting moments, hear the tune,
As night wraps all in sweet cocoon.

Timeless Melodies of the Sylvan Depths

Among the trees, where silence reigns,
Whispers echo, soft refrains.
The brook provides a gentle score,
While shadows play on forest floor.

Leaves rustle in a rhythmic dance,
Inviting all to take a chance.
Nature's choir sings from above,
Each note infused with endless love.

Glimmers of light through branches weave,
Creating magic, hard to believe.
A symphony of time stands still,
In these depths, all hearts can fill.

Moments linger, untraced by haste,
In every sound, a sweetened taste.
The forest hums with lore untold,
Melodies of ages old.

Listen closely to what it shares,
The heartbeats caught in whispered airs.
Timeless tunes, forever bound,
In the sylvan depths, magic found.

A Dance of Shadows and Light

When twilight fades and day departs,
The earth awakes, as beats of hearts.
Shadows mingle with soft glow,
A dance begins, a gentle flow.

Figures sway with secrets kept,
While moon above, the night has slept.
In the stillness, all unite,
To weave a tale through dark and light.

Dappled beams create the stage,
As whispers turn on every page.
In this realm where dreams take flight,
The dance of shadows shares its light.

Moments twirl as silence breathes,
Threading stories through autumn leaves.
With every step, the world unfurls,
A canvas painted in soft swirls.

So come and join this sacred trance,
Where night unfolds in tender glance.
In every leap and graceful turn,
The heart discovers what it yearns.

Lost Harmonies of the Enchanted Woods

In the depths of ancient trees,
Whispers drift on gentle breeze.
Once there thrived a symphony,
Now echoes fade in memory.

Mossy paths of muted cries,
Where magic danced beneath the skies.
Each note a dream, now scattered wide,
In silent glades where shadows bide.

Faded songs of joy and strife,
Painting tales of woodland life.
With every rustle, hints remain,
Of laughter lost, of love and pain.

Though time has claimed the serenade,
This forest holds the dreams we've made.
In twilight's glow, they softly rise,
In whispers sent to starry skies.

So take a moment, breathe it in,
The lost harmonies that lie within.
For in the woods, where spirits creep,
The melodies of memories sleep.

Melodies of the Forgotten Hollow

In whispers soft, the echoes play,
Through ancient trees, they drift away.
A chorus lost in twilight's glow,
Where time stands still, and secrets flow.

The brook hums low, a quiet tune,
Beneath the watchful, silver moon.
Each note a story, long concealed,
In hidden paths, their fate revealed.

The shadows dance in harmony,
With every rustle, wild and free.
Through mossy floors and tangled vines,
The hollow sings of ancient signs.

A breeze brings forth the woodland's sigh,
As stars awaken in the sky.
They twinkle down on dreams once lost,
Their melodies, a gentle frost.

The echoes fade as dawn draws near,
Yet in the heart, they'll linger here.
For those who seek the whispered call,
Will find the songs in every thrall.

Among the Moonlit Petals

In gardens where the shadows play,
The flowers bloom at close of day.
Their colors bright in silver light,
A dance of dreams, soft and slight.

Each petal holds a secret song,
A tale of love, where hearts belong.
The nightingale sings sweet and clear,
As whispers dance for all to hear.

The softest breeze stirs up the night,
Caressing blooms in pure delight.
In moonlit beams, their fragrance swirls,
Enchanting souls, the magic unfurls.

Among the petals, wishes grow,
In hues of pink, and azure glow.
They beckon softly to the wise,
To gaze upon the starlit skies.

As night draws close, the petals fold,
Preserving dreams that dare be told.
In slumber's arms, they'll find their way,
Till dawn arrives, to greet the day.

Songs of the Elfish Realm

In twilight's grip where shadows blend,
The elfin voices gently bend.
A harmony of laughs and sighs,
Beneath the veil of starlit skies.

They flit between the trees so tall,
In whispered secrets, they enthrall.
With silver wings, they roam the night,
In dances spun with pure delight.

Each song resounds, a playful tease,
With nature's pulse, they roam with ease.
Through sylvan glades and moonlit streams,
They weave the fabric of our dreams.

The fireflies join in gleeful flight,
In luminescent bursts, so bright.
Together they enchant the air,
With melodies beyond compare.

In every note, a spell is cast,
To anchor hearts and hold them fast.
For in this realm of magic's grace,
The elfish songs embrace the space.

Whimsical Waves of the Verdant Grotto

In emerald depths where shadows play,
The waters weave a bright ballet.
With every splash, a giggle flows,
As mystery in silence grows.

The rocks are dressed in mossy green,
Reflecting dreams that once have been.
A tranquil hum, the grotto's sigh,
Beneath the vast and limitless sky.

Rippling laughter, a playful tease,
The whispers travel with the breeze.
In every wave, a story spins,
Of joyful start and peaceful ends.

Beyond the light of sun-kissed streams,
Lie tales of wanderers' wild dreams.
Within the depths, the heart finds rest,
Amidst the nature's loving chest.

As shadows stretch and twilight falls,
The grotto beckons, softly calls.
In whimsical waves, the soul will glide,
Embracing peace where dreams abide.

Woven Whispers among the Leaves

In the hush of twilight's grace,
Soft rustles fill the air,
Branches sway with gentle ease,
Nature's secrets laid bare.

Moonlight weaves through emerald boughs,
Casting dreams beneath each shade,
Where whispers blend with evening sounds,
And time itself seems swayed.

The echoes dance on twilight's breath,
A symphony of sighs and tunes,
In shadows deep, the heart will rest,
Beneath the silvered moons.

Rustling tales of days gone by,
In every leaf, a story tucked,
Whispers call as starlight gleams,
Unraveled dreams, forever struck.

Eager hearts in silence link,
Beneath the canopy so wide,
In woven whispers, thoughts will sink,
Together, we shall bide.

Enchanted Chords of the Starry Night

Stars awaken in the dark,
A melody of distant light,
Echoes of the cosmos sing,
In chords that twinkle bright.

The nightingale's soft song begins,
A serenade for weary souls,
Underneath the velvet sky,
Where dreams and starlight strolls.

Each constellation holds a tale,
In whispers carried on the breeze,
A harmony of heartbeats felt,
As shadows waltz through trees.

Celestial notes entwine in flight,
In a dance that knows no end,
The universe, with tender grace,
Becomes our faithful friend.

In every gaze, a spark ignites,
As hearts align with cosmic fate,
Enchanted chords light up the night,
With love that never waits.

Lullaby of the Verdant Shadows

In the hush of twilight's glow,
Soft sighs cradle gentle leaf,
Nature whispers sweet and low,
Bringing solace, bringing peace.

Cocooned in the forest's arms,
Where shadows weave their sleepy song,
The world retreats, with all its charms,
In this realm where thoughts belong.

Crickets chirp a lullaby,
As fireflies dance in the night,
In this tender, soothing sigh,
Dreams take flight, bathed in light.

The breeze carries a whispered tune,
Through branches, soft as silken threads,
In harmony with the moon,
As weary hearts find their beds.

Lullabies of green enfold,
In arms of peace where troubles cease,
A song of life, tender and bold,
In verdant shades, we find our peace.

Soundscapes of the Faerie Realm

In twilight's glow, the faeries play,
Their laughter twirls in the mist,
From flower to flower, they flit and sway,
In a world where magic exists.

Whispers float on the gentle breeze,
A symphony of unseen grace,
In hidden nooks where shadows tease,
Time's embrace, a sweet embrace.

Mushrooms glow with a beckoning light,
As crickets strum on silver strings,
The faerie lights, a sparkling sight,
In harmony, their laughter rings.

Through fields where dappled sunlight streams,
Their voices twine with the rustling leaves,
Crafting a world stitched from dreams,
Where imagination believes.

Echoes linger on the air,
As dusk envelops the quiet glade,
In soundscapes rich, beyond compare,
The faerie realm serenely played.

Songs from the Elders of the Woodlands

In the shadow of towering trees,
Whispers dance upon the breeze.
Ancient tales in bark and leaf,
Heartfelt songs of joy and grief.

From roots deep in the earth they sing,
Echoes of life in every spring.
In twilight's embrace, strength is found,
Harmony woven through the ground.

Glimmers of wisdom, softly shared,
Under the sky, all hearts laid bare.
The forest holds its secrets tight,
In every rustling, stories ignite.

A melody of ages past,
In every gust, the shadows cast.
With every note, a tale unfolds,
Of warriors brave and lives retold.

Through seasons change, the songs endure,
Binding all souls with love so pure.
As twilight falls, the elders sway,
In luminous night, their voices play.

Mysteries Encased in Melodic Resonance

In a realm where shadows dwell,
Each note a secret, cast a spell.
Harmonies drift on the cool night air,
Unveiling dreams for those who dare.

The moonlight weaves a tapestry bright,
Strings of fate in the dark of night.
Voices raised in sweet refrain,
Awakening magic from hidden pain.

Rhythms pulse like a heartbeat found,
Whispering truths, hidden and unbound.
Echoes of laughter blend with sighs,
Melding in tune beneath starry skies.

Each chorus wraps around the heart,
Binding the listener, worlds apart.
Lost in the cadence, we drift along,
Carried by tides of an ancient song.

Notes fall like raindrops on thirsty ground,
Revealing secrets that long astound.
In melodic waves, mysteries glide,
Holding the universe tucked inside.

Murmurs of the Celestial Voyage

Stars awaken in the vast unknown,
Carrying dreams in their silent tone.
Cosmic whispers on a gentle breeze,
Guiding the hearts that ache to seize.

Galaxies twirl in a timeless dance,
Awakening souls through a cosmic trance.
Infinite journeys unfold with grace,
A tapestry woven in endless space.

Celestial currents, energies bright,
Illuminate paths through the dark of night.
Each heartbeat syncs with the pulse of time,
A universal rhythm, soothing and sublime.

The vastness beckons, calls out our name,
In the depths of wonder, none feel the same.
With each starlit breath, we embark anew,
Together we sail through the astral view.

Murmurs of love in the cosmic sea,
Eternal connections where spirits flee.
A voyage of light through the heavens above,
Guided by whispers of infinite love.

Treetop Serenades in the Dusk

As the sun sinks low, the treetops sigh,
Songs of the evening drift soft and high.
Rustling branches hum a gentle tune,
Crickets join in beneath the moon.

Lanterns of fireflies blink and glow,
Painting the night with a magical show.
Whispers of leaves create a soft breeze,
Telling tales as they sway with ease.

Nights filled with dreams under the stars,
Dancing in rhythm with echoes from afar.
Melodies blend, weaving hope and cheer,
In treetop concerts, the heart feels near.

The forest hums in a lullaby trance,
Inviting all creatures to join the dance.
Harmony wraps the world in its arms,
A symphony sung with nature's charms.

When dusk falls gently with a loving touch,
The woods embrace us, oh so much.
In treetop serenades, dreams take flight,
Beneath the stars' watchful, guiding light.

Arcane Echoes of the Mystic Wild

Beneath the moon's soft glow, they speak,
Whispers of secrets, shadows sleek.
The trees sway gently, tales unfold,
In twilight's arms, their stories told.

A dance of spirits, night enfolds,
Through ancient woods, enchantment molds.
With every step, the magic swirls,
In woven dreams, the heart unfurls.

Veils of mist embrace the night,
Awakening stars, a silvery light.
The silence hums with vibrant lore,
As echoes linger, forevermore.

In this domain of shadowed grace,
Time stands still, a timeless place.
Where nature sings a haunting tune,
In harmony with the silver moon.

Lost in wonder, I wander far,
Guided softly by each bright star.
In mystic wilds, my spirit flies,
Embracing magic that never dies.

Chords of the Celestial Canopy

In the night sky, a symphony hums,
Stars aligned, the cosmos drums.
Notes of starlight dance and twine,
Creating melodies so divine.

The wind carries whispers of old,
Stories of love, secrets untold.
Underneath the endless expanse,
Each glance a brief, eternal chance.

Galaxies spin in graceful play,
Harmonies rise to greet the day.
Beneath this vast, celestial stage,
Every heart becomes a page.

Drifting through dreams, the echoes soar,
Touched by wonders, we crave for more.
Each heartbeat syncs with the light,
In chords of joy, through the night.

As meteors streak and planets gleam,
Awakening us from the sweetest dream.
We dance beneath this starlit dome,
In chords of love, we find our home.

Harmonies that Lure the Wandering Heart

A gentle breeze calls through the trees,
Carrying whispers like melodies.
It stirs the spirit, a tender sigh,
Inviting the soul to wander high.

In twilight's glow, paths softly glow,
Where secrets beckon, and rivers flow.
Every step taken, a chance to find,
The music within, sweet and unconfined.

With each note played, the heart expands,
Guided by fate, through magical lands.
The wildflowers sway, keeping time,
Syncopated rhythms, nature sublime.

A chorus of stars, above so bright,
Cast dreams like spells, beneath the night.
Lost in the beauty, I dance and twirl,
In harmonies deep, my heart begins to swirl.

Through valleys of echo and peaks of light,
The wandering heart takes gentle flight.
Chasing the music, free and unbound,
In every heartbeat, a love profound.

Fantasies Wrapped in Gossamer Threads

In dawn's embrace, dream whispers weave,
Gossamer threads, in colors believe.
They shimmer softly, a magical sight,
Weaving tales of love and light.

A tapestry spun from wishes and dreams,
Where each golden thread silently gleams.
In fluttering hues, the stories swirl,
Crafting fantasies as time unfurls.

Through a landscape painted in pastel shade,
Each moment a spark, uniquely made.
The air is thick with possibilities,
As laughter drifts like whispers in the breeze.

Cascading visions, a garden of light,
Where every fantasy takes its flight.
In the depths of wonder, we lose control,
Wrapped in the magic that fills the soul.

From dawn till dusk, these dreams will play,
Guiding our hearts through night and day.
In fantasies wrapped, we find our way,
Through the gossamer threads, forever stay.

Lyrical Shadows of the Enchanted Glen

In the glen where soft winds sigh,
Whispers of dreams dance on by.
Shadows merge with the fading light,
Echoes of day yield to night.

Trees stand tall, guardians wise,
Underneath the vast, dark skies.
Moonlight drapes a silvery sheet,
Curled in the arms of the quiet street.

Crickets chirp their evening song,
As fireflies flicker, move along.
Nature hums with gentle grace,
In this hidden, timeless place.

Ferns sway soft in the cool night air,
While secrets linger everywhere.
A rustling leaf, a soft-spun thread,
Binding stories yet unsaid.

In the stillness where shadows play,
Hearts intertwine, come what may.
The glen whispers tales of old,
Of love, of life, of dreams untold.

Harmonies of the Woodland Spirits

In the woodland, melodies rise,
Spirits dance beneath the skies.
Leaves clap gently, soft and light,
In harmony with fading light.

Branches sway in rhythmic flow,
Guided by the breezes low.
Creatures join in nature's song,
Finding where they all belong.

Echoes drift through tree and glade,
Life's sweet music softly played.
Squirrels chatter, owls take flight,
Woodland spirits share the night.

Starlit pathways, dreams unfold,
Whispers of the wise and old.
Ancient trees with stories weave,
Intertwined in hearts that believe.

In every rustle, every call,
Nature's symphony enthralls.
Together in this sacred space,
Woodland spirits find their place.

Serenade beneath the Starry Canopy

Underneath the twinkling sky,
Dreams take flight, and wishes fly.
Stars like candles brightly glow,
Illuminating paths we know.

Whispers carried by the breeze,
Through the branches of the trees.
Nighttime crickets serenade,
In the moonlight, shadows played.

A silver river flows above,
Woven threads of light and love.
Each constellation tells a tale,
Of love that journeys without fail.

Nature sways in rhythmic trance,
As the night invites a dance.
Hearts unite beneath the glow,
In the magic that we know.

With every glance at starlit view,
Promises are born anew.
In this serenade so bright,
We find peace within the night.

Chime of the Morning Dew

Morning breaks with softest hue,
Nature wakes, the world feels new.
Dewdrops sparkle, diamonds fall,
Whispers of the dawn's sweet call.

Birds unveil their songs of cheer,
As sunshine draws the shadows near.
Petals open, fresh and bright,
Kissing the warmth of morning light.

Fields adorned in glistening beads,
Nourishing the waking seeds.
Every leaf, a gleaming view,
In the magic of the dew.

The brook hums a gentle tune,
Echoing the sun and moon.
Nature's breath, a sacred space,
Where all find their rightful place.

As the day begins to rise,
In this world of tranquil sighs,
Chimes of morning, pure and true,
Awakening the heart anew.

Captivating Lyricism in the Twilight Mist

Whispers dance in fading light,
Soft shadows cradle the night.
Stars begin their gentle glow,
As twilight weaves a tale below.

Echoes shimmer in the breeze,
Nature's heart begins to seize.
A melody both light and deep,
Where dreams and waking worlds seep.

Through the mist, a voice calls clear,
The mysteries of dusk draw near.
Every sigh, a secret spun,
In the twilight, all is one.

Colors shift, the canvas fades,
Life cascades through velvet glades.
In each moment, magic stirs,
Capturing hearts in silent purrs.

As shadows bloom and days decline,
The world awaits the next design.
In twilight's arms, forever bound,
A captivating love is found.

Reverberations of the Elder Trees

Ancient limbs reach for the sky,
Roots of wisdom, strong and spry.
Tales of yore they softly share,
In rustling leaves, a timeless air.

Each ring, a story deeply sown,
Of seasons passed, of seeds once blown.
Their bark, a canvas worn yet grand,
Whispers echo across the land.

With every gust, a voice profound,
In rustles, life is woven sound.
Branches sway, a graceful plea,
In harmony, they breathe to be.

Beneath the shade, a world awakes,
Life in shadows, dreams it makes.
Elder trees with arms outspread,
Cradle secrets long since said.

In reverberations, truth remains,
Nature's heart in soft refrains.
With every echo, memories bound,
In elder trees, our roots are found.

Lyrical Dreams in the Enchanted Thicket

In the thicket, shadows breathe,
Where dreams lie gently underneath.
A symphony of night unfolds,
In whispered tones, the magic holds.

Moonlit paths weave tales anew,
Mysteries wrapped in silver dew.
Every rustle, a secret song,
Inviting souls to come along.

Stars glimmer through the branches' lace,
A magical and timeless space.
In lyrical dances, hearts take flight,
Through enchanted realms of night.

With each step, the world transforms,
In gentle waves, the spirit warms.
Nature's voice, a tender sigh,
In the thicket, we learn to fly.

As dawn tiptoes through the mist,
Morning's glow, a dreamer's tryst.
In the thicket, all is free,
Where lyrical dreams find their glee.

A Forest's Breath and Time's Melody

A forest breathes, a timeless song,
In every leaf, where dreams belong.
Nature's heart beats slow and pure,
In golden light, all souls endure.

Sunlight dapples on the floor,
A symphony of peace in store.
With each rustle, stories play,
In harmony, they find their way.

Time whispers softly 'neath the boughs,
Reminding us of sacred vows.
A life unfolds as shadows blend,
In nature's arms, we find a friend.

Every branch, a note so sweet,
Guiding us with rhythmic beat.
In this embrace, our worries cease,
In the forest, time finds peace.

A melody of earth and sky,
Intertwined as moments fly.
With every breath, a story told,
In the forest's heart, we grow bold.

Mystical Melodies Among the Woodland Spirits

In the shadows where whispers dwell,
The spirits dance with a silent swell.
Moonlight glimmers on leaves aglow,
Creating a symphony soft and slow.

Elms sway gently, the breeze a guide,
Nature's chorus, where secrets bide.
Each note a tale, each rustle a song,
In this realm where dreams belong.

Ancient echoes through branches soar,
Calling the lost, they return once more.
A lullaby hums in the cool night air,
Binding enchantments beyond compare.

Within this thicket, time stands still,
The heart of the forest, a magic thrill.
Footsteps echo on mossy ground,
As nature's melodies weave around.

So listen closely, let your heart believe,
The woodland spirits have tales to weave.
In mystical melodies, find your way,
To the magic that dances by night and day.

Harmonies in the Elfin Thicket

Beneath the boughs where fairies dwell,
A harmony rings like a ringing bell.
Glimmers of laughter, whispers of light,
Echo the secrets of day and night.

Petals open, revealing a dance,
As woodland creatures share a glance.
The rhythm of nature sets hearts ablaze,
In this enchanted thicket, we fade and graze.

Mossy carpets beneath our feet,
Conducting a symphony both soft and sweet.
Gentle winds carry dreams afar,
While moonbeams wrap us in a silvery star.

The elfin light casts shadows long,
A place where our spirits sing and throng.
Unseen voices beckon us near,
Creating a harmony we long to hear.

In the thicket, magic intertwines,
A melody born where daylight shines.
Together we lift our hearts in glee,
In this elfin realm, forever free.

The Song of the Hidden Glade

Where sunlight dapples the forest floor,
A hidden glade opens, a sacred door.
The air hums sweet with a timeless tune,
As flowers sway 'neath the watchful moon.

Whispers of ivy and rustling leaves,
Weave through branches where no heart grieves.
Each heartbeat thrums with the pulse of the earth,
In this tranquil haven, we find rebirth.

Crickets serenade, a rhythmic sound,
The essence of peace in this magic ground.
Nature's orchestra plays soft and low,
As gaze meets gaze, lost in the flow.

With every breeze, a story unfolds,
In the hidden glade, ancient and bold.
Murmurs and sighs intertwine like vines,
Creating a ballad that forever shines.

So pause for a moment, let your heart sway,
In the song of the glade, let worries decay.
For in silent whispers of nature's embrace,
We discover the beauty of time's gentle grace.

Enchanted Chimes of the Forest Heart

In the heart of the forest, where time stands still,
Enchanted chimes echo with a gentle thrill.
Each note a flutter, a silvery call,
Reverberating softly, the magic enthralls.

Boughs sway lightly, a whispering breeze,
Caressing the trunks of the ancient trees.
As laughter dances on the shimmering air,
The forest heart sings with a tune so rare.

Glimmers of sunlight through leaves cascade,
Turning the darkness into a grand parade.
Crystals of dewdrop, each shimmering light,
Join in the chorus as day turns to night.

Moss-covered stones keep secrets untold,
Within their shadows, the forest grows bold.
A gentle reminder of nature's sweet art,
In enchanted chimes, we find our heart.

So linger a while, let the music flow,
In the depths of the woods where soft breezes blow.
Let the chimes guide you to realms unknown,
In the forest heart, we are never alone.

Whispers in the Moonlit Glade

In the hush of night, shadows sway,
Moonbeams dance where fairies play.
Leaves murmur secrets, old and wise,
While stars twinkle in velvet skies.

Gentle breezes carry soft sighs,
Rustling grass where magic lies.
Midnight blooms with glowing light,
Embrace the calm of this lovely night.

A brook babbles tales long forgotten,
By flowers kissed, and dreams begotten.
Silence wraps the slumbering earth,
Cradling each whisper, each rebirth.

Crickets serenade the gentle night,
While shadows flicker, soft and light.
In this glade, where spirits roam,
Every whisper feels like home.

As the moon sets, magic fades,
Leaving traces of its glades.
But in the heart, the echoes stay,
Of whispers made in night's ballet.

Chords of Enchantment in the Sylvan Hollow

In the sylvan hollow, music flows,
From hidden nooks where wildflowers grow.
Each note dances on the breeze,
Bringing calm, inviting ease.

Violin song from branches high,
Where larks and sparrows soar and fly.
The rustle of leaves joins the tune,
As whispers fade beneath the moon.

Harmony woven in nature's art,
Plays gently on the listener's heart.
Mossy stones and ancient trees,
Reflect the magic in the leaves.

Echoes linger, a sweet refrain,
Each note touched by the summer rain.
Songs of yesteryears softly call,
In this hollow, enchanting all.

When twilight falls, the music swells,
Rippling through the forest's spells.
Safe in the arms of nature's song,
In sylvan hollow, where I belong.

Echoes of the Faerie's Laughter

In the glimmer of dawn, laughter sings,
Through the trees, where joy takes wing.
Faeries dance on petals fair,
Spreading delight in the cool spring air.

Glistening dewdrops, a radiant shower,
Reflect the joy in every flower.
With giggles bright, they weave their thread,
In every heart, joy is bred.

Arm in arm, they twirl and sway,
In meadows where sunlight plays.
Their echoes float on fragrant breeze,
Caressing blooms and rustling leaves.

As twilight falls, their laughter blends,
With whispers of night as daylight ends.
In every shadow, magic thrives,
In echoes of laughter, the faerie lives.

To dream of faeries, joy unbound,
In each soft chuckle, enchantment's found.
The world awakens, kissed by flight,
In echoes of laughter, pure delight.

Melodies from the Hidden Grove

In the hidden grove, where secrets dwell,
Nature plays her timeless spell.
A symphony of rustling leaves,
Fills the air as daylight weaves.

Birdsong threads through branches wide,
With whispering winds, they dance and glide.
Melodies born from a heart so deep,
Awake the forest from its sleep.

The brook joins in with a bubbling tune,
Reflecting harmony beneath the moon.
Sunlight dapples the soft, green ground,
While magic in every note is found.

In this grove, the spirits play,
Guiding hearts that have lost their way.
Echoing laughter, gentle and bright,
In this hidden world, pure delight.

As twilight drapes its starry veil,
Melodies linger, never pale.
Each memory held, like a soft embrace,
In the hidden grove, a cherished place.

Dreams Woven in Fairy Dust

In the twilight's shimmering glow,
Dreams weave through silver streams,
Fairies dance on petals soft,
Carrying the night's sweet dreams.

Glistening wings in moonlight sway,
Whispers of secrets float on air,
Each twirl a soft, gentle sigh,
Laughter echoes, light and rare.

Stars peek through the emerald leaves,
The forest hums a lullaby,
Crickets join in with their song,
As shadows dart and spirits fly.

Magic lingers, tender and bright,
In the heart of the sleeping glade,
Where wishes blossom, taking flight,
In dreams, our hopes are made.

So let us weave a world of light,
With threads of whispers and delight,
In the fabric of night's embrace,
We'll find our dreams, our sacred place.

Luminous Harmonies of the Night Sky

Stars shimmer with secrets untold,
As night wraps the world in a hug,
The moon sings a lullaby bright,
In this cosmic dance, we snug.

Planets twirl, a silent ballet,
Comets streak with trails of fire,
Galaxies hum in soft, sweet tones,
Awakening our heart's desire.

In the cool breeze, whispers fly,
Holding the echoes of the past,
Each twinkle a tale, a mystery,
A harmony destined to last.

Crickets chirp in rhythmic bliss,
Their serenade a soothing balm,
While dreams play peek-a-boo above,
In this tranquil, celestial calm.

So let's dance under skies of grace,
In luminous harmonies we trust,
The night whispers sweet, soft truths,
As we find solace in stardust.

Shadows Danced in Melodic Rapture

Where shadows fade and whispers blend,
In gardens where secrets remain,
The night breathes softly, full of grace,
Melodies swirl like gentle rain.

Beneath the stars, we sway and spin,
The air is thick with sweet perfume,
As shadows dance, they twirl and glide,
In the darkness, they break the gloom.

With every step, the world feels right,
The moonlight kisses tender skin,
We lose ourselves in sound and light,
Where every heart begins to sing.

Thumping beats in whispered tones,
The night ignites the fire within,
Together we weave vibrant tales,
In this rapture, our souls begin.

So let us dance till morning's light,
Where shadows play and spirits soar,
In melodic dreams together we fly,
Forever yearning, forevermore.

The Enigma of Elven Whispers

In twilight glades where silence reigns,
Elven whispers softly thread,
Secrets linger on the breeze,
A tapestry of thoughts unsaid.

Moonlit paths where shadows creep,
Every glance a story spun,
In the heart of ancient woods,
The elven song has just begun.

With every rustle, every sigh,
Nature hums the sacred lore,
Calling forth the brave and bold,
To unravel the myths of yore.

Mysteries wrapped in silver mist,
With each echo, magic thrives,
The forest breathes enchanted dreams,
In whispers, the old world survives.

So step lightly, hear their song,
In every shadow, light appears,
The enigma of elven whispers,
Awakening our hopes and fears.

Lullabies for the Wandering Fey

In moonlit glades where shadows play,
The wandering fey drift soft away.
With whispers sweet as summer's breeze,
They dance among the swaying trees.

Through twilight's veil, their laughter rings,
A song of night, of hidden things.
Crickets hum in harmony,
As stars adorn the canopy.

Each gentle sigh, the brook's embrace,
In nature's arms, they find their place.
With every note, their spirits soar,
They weave the dreams forevermore.

The flowers bend to hear the tune,
Under the watchful, silver moon.
And in the stillness of the night,
The fey's lullaby takes flight.

A gift of peace, a fleeting glance,
In every heart, they spark a dance.
As night unfolds, they drift away,
Till dawn arrives to greet the day.

Whimsical Rhythms of the Secret Copse

In shady nooks where secrets dwell,
The trees unfold their leafy shell.
A symphony of rustling leaves,
Where every creature softly weaves.

The brook gurgles with playful cheer,
As fairies flit, so light and mere.
With twinkling eyes and flitting wings,
They dance to nature's gentle sings.

A melody of whispers soft,
In all the branches, spirits loft.
The owl hoots low, the night's embrace,
Each chorus echoes in this place.

With silver beams of starlit grace,
The world slows down, a sacred space.
Where time stands still, and worries flee,
In rhythms known by you and me.

The copse invites with open arms,
To share its secrets, healing charms.
As laughter mingles with the night,
We lose ourselves in pure delight.

Songs of the Forest's Heart

Beneath the boughs where shadows stir,
The forest hums a gentle purr.
Each rustle speaks of ancient lore,
In every hue, the spirits soar.

The thrush sings out a morning tune,
While dew-kissed blooms greet the soft noon.
A chorus of life in radiant throng,
The heart of the woods is alive and strong.

Crimson leaves in their golden fall,
Whisper secrets, a silent call.
The breeze carries dreams along the way,
As twilight ushers in the play.

In shadows deep, the night takes hold,
While moonlight weaves a tale retold.
Each star a note in the darkened sky,
A lullaby for the night to sigh.

Connected to every trace of earth,
The forest's pulse is filled with worth.
In every song, a piece of art,
A love letter from the forest's heart.

Mystical Murmurs of the Twilight Realm

In twilight hours, where dreams begin,
The realm of magic draws us in.
With whispers soft as evening air,
Mystical murmurs linger there.

The fog rolls in with secrets new,
As shadows dance in shades of blue.
A glimpse of light in a hidden glen,
Inviting those who roam within.

With every rustle, there's a tale,
Of wanderers who drift and sail.
The nightingale sings from deep within,
Where silence breathes, and echoes spin.

The moonlight spills on dewy grass,
As fleeting moments gently pass.
In dreams we find our way to roam,
In twilight's heart, we feel at home.

As stars align in their twinkling flight,
We find our path through the silent night.
In whispers soft, the world reveals,
The magic that the twilight feels.

The Vermilion Chorus of the Emerging Dawn

The sky ignites in fiery hues,
Birdsong breaks the morning calm.
Shadows retreat from light's embrace,
A symphony of hope, a balm.

Golden rays kiss every leaf,
Awakening dreams once lost.
The world begins its gentle dance,
In warmth, all fears are tossed.

Whispers of the rising sun,
Tell tales of joy and peace.
Nature sings in pure delight,
As night's soft grip will cease.

Crimson hues blend with blue skies,
Life emerges, bright and bold.
Every moment a precious gift,
A story waiting to be told.

In this chorus, hearts unite,
With each note like a spark.
Together we embrace the dawn,
In harmony, we find our mark.

A Tapestry of Tones in the Emerald Canopy

Beneath the leaves, a soft refrain,
Nature's whispers weave through trees.
Gentle breezes carry songs,
A melody that brings us ease.

Gold and green in light's embrace,
Dappled shadows dancing free.
Every rustle tells a tale,
Of secrets kept in memory.

Birds in flight, their voices blend,
In harmony, they weave the air.
With every note, the forest hums,
A rhythm flowing everywhere.

Sunbeams filter, warming ground,
Life awakens with a smile.
In this emerald world so rich,
We linger, savoring a while.

The canopy, a shelter safe,
Embracing hearts beneath its shade.
In this moment, we are whole,
In nature's song, our fears do fade.

Invocations of the Hidden Grove

In shadowed realms, soft echoes rise,
Mysteries wrapped in twilight's glow.
Whispers call from ancient trees,
Where time and magic intertwine slow.

The ground is cool, the air is thick,
With secrets held by leaves above.
Each step unfolds another tale,
A world embraced by peace and love.

Crickets chirp a soothing song,
As night descends in velvet grace.
The grove awakens with each sound,
In its embrace, we find our place.

Stars ignite on darkness' canvas,
A tapestry of dreams and sight.
In this space of sacred whispers,
Our souls take flight into the night.

Beneath the moon, we seek the truth,
The hidden grove reveals its heart.
In silent vows and tender breaths,
We find the magic in the dark.

Fluttering Chimes of Midnight Bliss

As shadows wrap the world in hush,
The moonlight drapes a silver thread.
Each breath we take, a quiet song,
In twilight's arms, our worries shed.

Crickets play their softest tune,
A serenade for healing hearts.
The stars twinkle, a dance of light,
Guiding us to peaceful parts.

Gentle breezes sway the trees,
Like whispers shared among old friends.
Every sound a fleeting gift,
With every note, the darkness bends.

In this realm, the spirits sing,
Fluttering chimes of midnight's grace.
A lullaby of dreams and hopes,
In stillness, we find our place.

Awake, yet lost in sweet embrace,
We drift in moments soft and bright.
As dawn approaches, we shall rise,
Transformed by this enchanting night.

Echoing Howl of the Whispering Pines

In shadows deep where whispers wane,
The pines converse in soft refrain.
Their echoes stretch across the night,
Carried forth on silvered light.

A howl floats through the tender trees,
Dancing with the playful breeze.
An ancient story, lost but near,
Guided by the moon's bright sphere.

Ghostly shadows weave and twine,
Nature's song a haunting line.
The branches sway in solemn grace,
Holding secrets time can't erase.

Veils of mist drape low and thin,
Where silence breathes and dreams begin.
Each note a thread of time and space,
In the forest's warm embrace.

When dawn emerges, calm and bright,
The echoes fade, retreat from sight.
Yet in our hearts, forever stay,
The whispers of the night's ballet.

Dreamscapes in Moonlit Boughs

Beneath the boughs, the shadows play,
Crafting dreams to chase away.
Moonlit trails invite the wanderer,
To find what lies in evening's armor.

Softly glowing, the silver beams,
Kiss the leaves, like tender dreams.
Each branch a cradle, every sigh,
A lullaby for those who fly.

In twilight's hush, the magic swirls,
Through the hearts of boys and girls.
A symphony of peace and light,
Guiding souls through gentle night.

Within this realm, the stars align,
Tales unfold, entwine divine.
Here, where wishes breathe and bloom,
The forest hums a sleepy tune.

As dawn paints skies with hues anew,
The dreams will fade, but memories glue.
In every heart a spark will yield,
The magic found within the field.

The Forest's Heartbeat Beneath the Canopy

A rhythm pulses, strong and deep,
Within the woods, a secret keep.
The heartbeat drums beneath the roots,
In silent whispers, life rebutes.

Branches arch in graceful span,
Cradling tales of earth and man.
Leaves murmur soft in morning's light,
Speaking life in spirits bright.

Among the trunks, where shadows creep,
The echoing silence does not sleep.
Voices linger, laughter shared,
In this realm, where hearts have dared.

Through the canopy, sunlight streams,
Awakening the forest's dreams.
Each creature stirs, each leaf aglow,
In harmony, the wild does flow.

As twilight descends, the heartbeat slows,
A lullaby in twilight's throes.
Yet in the night, strong memories nest,
In the woods' embrace, we find our rest.

Ethereal Chants of the Glimmering Glade

In the glade where fireflies gleam,
Ethereal voices weave a dream.
A chorus soft, of night's delight,
Whispers echo, under starlit night.

With every shimmer, a tale unfolds,
Of ancient magic, and spirits bold.
The twilight dances, shadows sway,
In harmony, as night turns gray.

The cool breeze carries sweet refrain,
Through dew-kissed grass, where dreams remain.
With each note, the silence grieves,
For all the tales the heart believes.

Wandering souls in wonder roam,
Finding solace far from home.
In this abode where echoes twine,
Nature's song forever shine.

As dawn approaches, the melodies fade,
Yet linger still, in hearts displayed.
The glade holds magic, pure and bright,
In every memory, a spark of light.

Fable in Whispers of the Wood

In the heart of the grove, stories unfold,
Leaves gently murmur, secrets retold.
Branches weave tales of the old and the new,
In whispers of green, dreams take their cue.

The shadows dance lightly, draped on the ground,
While echoes of laughter in breezes abound.
Creatures of twilight, with glimmers of grace,
Join in the chorus, a soft, sweet embrace.

Moonlight spills silver, on carpet of moss,
Painting the night, where hope finds its gloss.
The fables we share, in this secretive wood,
Are woven in laughter, understood and good.

Vibrant Echoes of Nature's Canvas

In the dawn's gentle light, colors ignite,
Flowers bloom boldly, a glorious sight.
Each petal a brushstroke, vivid and bright,
Nature's own palette, a pure delight.

Birds sing with fervor, melodies soar,
Their vibrant tunes echo, forevermore.
Leaves sway to the rhythm, a lively ballet,
In this canvas of life, joy leads the way.

Streams glisten softly, reflecting the skies,
Rippling with laughter, where serenity lies.
Each moment a masterpiece, painted with care,
Nature's own wonders, a love we can share.

Luminous Tones of the Hidden Pathway

A pathway unfolds in the hush of the night,
With luminous tones that dance in the light.
Moss underfoot, like a velvety dream,
Leads through the shadows, where starlight does gleam.

Each step feels enchanted, a journey so rare,
Whispers of magic hang thick in the air.
Crickets provide a sweet symphony's call,
As the soft glow of fireflies encircles us all.

In the depth of the forest, we wander and roam,
Finding our way, the pathway feels like home.
With each gentle breath, our hearts open wide,
In luminous tones, where the wonders abide.

Reverent Notes of the Elder Tree

The elder tree stands, ancient and wise,
Its branches like arms, reaching for skies.
In its embrace, the world feels at peace,
A refuge of solace, where worries cease.

With roots deep and sturdy, it anchors the earth,
Holding the stories of ages and birth.
Leaves rustle softly, like whispers in air,
Guardians of secrets, always aware.

In the dusk's warm embrace, shadows extend,
The elder tree hums, a faithful friend.
Reverent notes played, a timeless refrain,
In the heart of the woods, where love does remain.

Rhapsody of the Verdant Retreat

In emerald embrace, the shadows dance,
Whispers of nature, a delicate trance.
Beneath the boughs, the secrets lay,
Time drifts softly, fading away.

Dappled light filters through the trees,
Kissed by the breeze, a gentle tease.
Colors paint the ground with grace,
In this haven, I find my place.

A brook murmurs tales of yore,
Echoes of life, a sacred lore.
Each stone and petal sings a tune,
As twilight unfolds beneath the moon.

Mossy carpets where dreams take flight,
In the hush of dusk, the world feels right.
With every breath, the spirit soars,
In this retreat, my heart restores.

Beneath the stars, the air is sweet,
Nature's rhapsody, a rhythm discreet.
I linger here, in blissful sway,
In verdant arms, my soul will stay.

Ballad of the Glimmering Ferns

In the quiet glade, soft whispers breathe,
Glimmers of green, where the fairies weave.
Ferns unfurl in a tender embrace,
Nature's ballet, a timeless grace.

Sunlight dapples the verdant hue,
Each leaf a story, each drop a dew.
A symphony of life, brimming bright,
In this hidden realm, pure delight.

Crickets serenade the fading light,
Nightfall beckons, stars burn bright.
Glow of the moon, a touch so dear,
Guardian of dreams, drawing near.

With every rustle, the song prevails,
Nature's cadence tells enchanting tales.
The ferns, they shimmer, in silver glow,
A ballad sung where the wild winds blow.

In the heart of the woods, the echoes play,
Glimmering ferns lead the way.
Together we dance, in shadows cast,
In the song of the night, forever last.

Overture of the Dreamweaver's Realm

In the still of night, where dreams take flight,
A tapestry woven, rich and bright.
Stars whisper secrets in silken threads,
Guiding the way to the slumbering heads.

Laughter of stardust, a melodic flow,
As shadows of night weave a soft glow.
Wonders unfold in the dreamer's embrace,
Time dances slowly in this sacred space.

Visions unfurl like petals in spring,
A chorus of night, with the morning to bring.
Each heartbeat echoes, a story retold,
In the arms of the night, mysteries unfold.

In the dreamweaver's realm, lost and found,
Imagination's whispers surround.
A nightingale's song carries me high,
In the overtones of dreams, we fly.

Touched by the stars, the night deepens still,
A journey through realms, a wanderer's thrill.
With dreams as our guide, we are never alone,
In the overture's embrace, we've truly grown.

Symphonies of the Enchanted Thicket

Amidst the thicket, the symphony swells,
Nature's orchestra, casting its spells.
Leaves rustle gently in whispered sighs,
As laughter of sprites dances through the skies.

In shadows of twilight, the tune unfolds,
Serenading secrets that the forest holds.
With each note played, the heart takes wing,
In the enchanted depths, my spirit sings.

Crickets join in with rhythmic cheer,
Echoes of life that linger near.
The winds carry tales, both old and wise,
As stars awaken and illuminate the skies.

Every branch a melody, every stream a chord,
Nature, a canvas on which dreams are poured.
In this embrace, I find my home,
Amidst the symphonies, forever I roam.

Through the thicket's heart, the spirit flows,
Where time stands still and wonder grows.
In the chorus of night, I find my part,
In the enchanted thicket, I hear my heart.

www.ingramcontent.com/pod-product-compliance
Ingram Content Group UK Ltd.
Pitfield, Milton Keynes, MK11 3LW, UK
UKHW021638200125
4187UKWH00003B/182